The
CREATION
ST🌍RY

In Words and Sign Language

John P. Audia

Illustrated by David Spohn

LITURGICAL PRESS
Collegeville, Minnesota

www.litpress.org

The 1st Day

God created Heaven and Earth
for you and me.
Earth began in nothing
but darkness, wind, and sea.
Then Earth became bright
as God created light.

God   Created   Light

The 2ⁿᵈ Day

A dome appeared up high.
God created sky.
God's dome, blue as blue could be,
separated sky from mighty sea.

God

Created

Sky

The 3ʳᵈ Day

Gathering all waters with a mighty hand,
God gave us land.
God named it Earth and saw its need.
God said, "Every plant and fruit tree
must bear seed."

God

Gave

Land

The 4ᵗʰ Day

Beginning with a twinkling in the sky,
God created stars that burn up high.
God said, "Let moon lead night,
and sun guide day by giving light."

God

Created

Stars

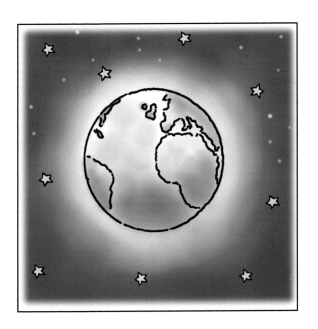

The 5th Day

Let waters fill with fish that swim by.
Let birds fly the heavens named sky.
Water, fish will call home.
Sky is where birds forever roam.

Birds

Fly

Heavens

The 6ᵗʰ Day

God said, "Let animals walk
my green ground,
each with their own special sound."
God said, "I'll create man and woman
in my image alone.
I'll love them forever as my own."

God

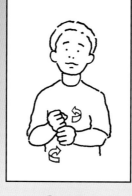

Created

People

The 7th Day

God rested and could see
Heaven and Earth,
a beautiful place to be.

God

Rested

1	2	3	4	5	6	7	8	9

Library of Congress Cataloging-in-Publication Data

Audia, John P.
 The creation story : in words and sign language / John P. Audia ;
illustrated by David Spohn.
  p. cm.
 ISBN-13: 978-0-8146-3174-4
 ISBN-10: 0-8146-3174-6
  1. Creation—Juvenile literature. 2. Bible stories, English—O.T.
Genesis. 3. Sign language—Juvenile literature. I. Spohn, David. II.
Title.

BS651.A785 2007
222'.1109505—dc22   2006031504